Made in United States
Troutdale, OR
12/08/2024

26039288R00066